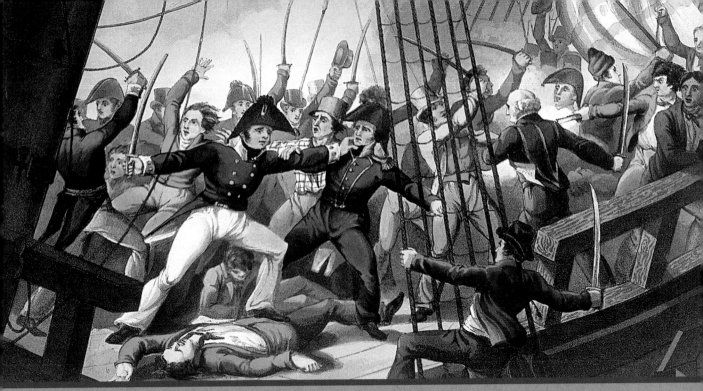

PRIMARY SOURCES IN AMERICAN HISTORY™

THE WAR OF 1812

A PRIMARY SOURCE HISTORY OF AMERICA'S SECOND WAR WITH BRITAIN

LIZ SONNEBORN

rosen central

Primary Source™

The Rosen Publishing Group, Inc., New York

Published in 2004 by The Rosen Publishing Group, Inc.
29 East 21st Street, New York, NY 10010

First Edition

Library of Congress Cataloging-in-Publication Data

Sonneborn, Liz.
The War of 1812 / by Liz Sonneborn.— 1st ed.
    v. cm. — (Primary sources in American history)
Includes bibliographical references and index.
Contents: The road to war—On land and on sea—Victory and defeat—Invading Washington—At peace.
ISBN 0-8239-4515-4 (library binding)
1. United States—History—War of 1812—Juvenile literature. [1. United States—History—War of 1812.] I. Title. II. Series.
E354.S66 2004
973.5'2–dc21

                                                                                    2003010602

Manufactured in the United States of America

On the front cover: the USS *Chesapeake* crippled by the HMS *Shannon*'s broadsides. Colored lithograph by L. Haghe after a painting by J. C. Schetky. Published in 1830. Courtesy of the U.S. Naval Academy Museum.

On the back cover: first row *(left to right)*: committee drafting the Declaration of Independence for action by the Continental Congress; Edward Braddock and troops ambushed by Indians at Fort Duquesne. Second row *(left to right)*: the Mayflower in Plymouth Harbor; the Oregon Trail at Barlow Cutoff. Third row *(left to right)*: slaves waiting at a slave market; the USS *Chesapeake* under fire from the HMS *Shannon*.

CONTENTS

NTRODUCTION

On June 1, 1812, President James Madison sent a message to the U.S. Congress. Its topic was England, then the United States's greatest enemy. Madison listed the many ways England had abused and insulted the nation. Eighteen days later, America's lawmakers responded to Madison's charges. Congress issued a declaration of war.

THE SECOND WAR OF INDEPENDENCE

The declaration began the War of 1812 (1812-1815). It was the second time the United States had gone to war with England. Almost thirty years earlier, Americans had battled the English in the American Revolution (1775-1783). Before that war, the English controlled the colonies of the Atlantic coast of America. After the Americans won the Revolution, they were able to establish their own independent nation.

Since the Revolution, however, England had not always respected the independence of the United States. Many Americans were particularly upset that England interfered with American trading ships. Congress agreed with President Madison that the only way to stop the English was to defeat them in battle again.

James Madison fought against England and France's capture of American ships when he served as secretary of state for Thomas Jefferson. After he was elected to the presidency in 1808, the situation had escalated, bringing about the need for the War of 1812. A president with deep belief in his nation, he wrote, "The advice nearest to my heart and deepest in my convictions is that the Union of the States be cherished and perpetuated."

As the War of 1812 began, the United States was still a very young country. Its army was small. Its navy had few ships. Its soldiers and sailors were inexperienced. England, on the other hand, had one of the world's greatest fighting forces.

In deciding to go to war, the United States was taking an enormous risk. If it won, the new nation would prove its ability to defend itself. But if it was defeated, the United States could lose its independence forever.

TIMELINE

June 18, 1812 — The United States declares war against Great Britain.

August 16, 1812 — General William Hull surrenders Fort Detroit to the English.

August 18, 1812 — American ship USS *Constitution* defeats the HMS *Guerrière* in a sea battle.

April 27, 1813 — American troops sack the Canadian town of York (now Toronto, Ontario).

June 1, 1813 — The HMS *Shannon* defeats the USS *Chesapeake*. American commander Captain James Lawrence tells crew, "Don't give up the ship" before dying.

September 10, 1813 — Commander Oliver Hazard Perry defeats an English fleet on Lake Erie.

October 5, 1813 — English and Indian force is defeated at the Battle of the Thames.

March 1814 — The Napoleonic Wars end, freeing England to send more soldiers to North America.

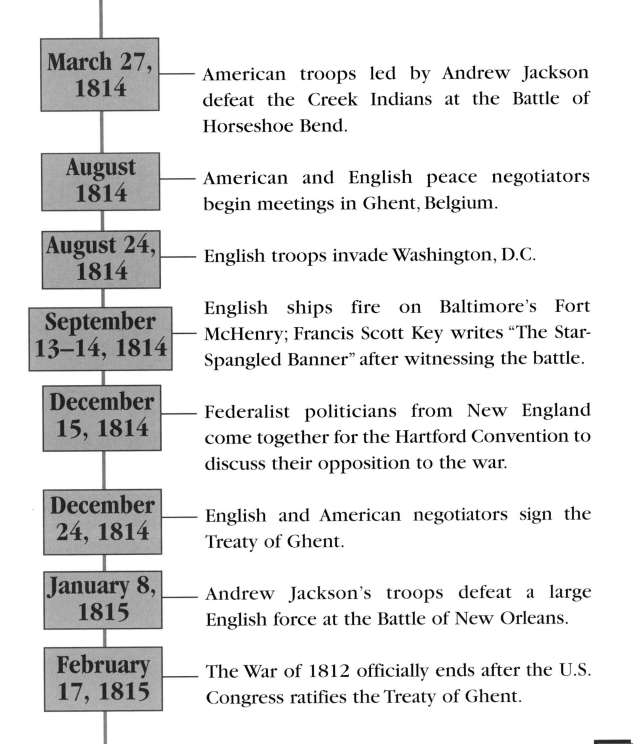

TIMELINE

March 27, 1814 — American troops led by Andrew Jackson defeat the Creek Indians at the Battle of Horseshoe Bend.

August 1814 — American and English peace negotiators begin meetings in Ghent, Belgium.

August 24, 1814 — English troops invade Washington, D.C.

September 13–14, 1814 — English ships fire on Baltimore's Fort McHenry; Francis Scott Key writes "The Star-Spangled Banner" after witnessing the battle.

December 15, 1814 — Federalist politicians from New England come together for the Hartford Convention to discuss their opposition to the war.

December 24, 1814 — English and American negotiators sign the Treaty of Ghent.

January 8, 1815 — Andrew Jackson's troops defeat a large English force at the Battle of New Orleans.

February 17, 1815 — The War of 1812 officially ends after the U.S. Congress ratifies the Treaty of Ghent.

CHAPTER 1

THE ROAD TO WAR

Soon after the American Revolution, the nation's leaders split into two political parties—the Federalists and the Republicans (also called the Democratic-Republicans). From 1789 to 1801, the Federalists were the party in power. Many Federalists were wealthy merchants and business owners. They believed in keeping the American economy strong. They also wanted to build up the country's army and navy. According to the Federalists, the United States needed a strong military, just in case it had to defend itself.

The Republicans disagreed. They resented having to pay taxes to finance a standing army. They said that if the country were attacked, it could rally plenty of volunteers to fight.

By 1800, the population was growing quickly. Most Americans were small farmers with little money to spare. They liked the Republicans' promise to cut taxes. With their support, the Republican presidential candidate, Thomas Jefferson, won that year's election. Almost immediately, he slashed the budget for the country's army and navy.

England and France at War

While the United States was dismantling its military, many countries in Europe were building theirs up. France was then ruled

The United States's third president, Thomas Jefferson, penned the Declaration of Independence, whose words are still memorized by most schoolchildren. Jefferson believed strongly in the principles that continue to be debated in the United States today, such as liberty, the separation of church and state, and states' rights.

by Napoléon I. He sent French troops all over Europe, hoping to conquer the entire continent, country by country.

Napoléon took over much of the continent. But he had trouble getting a foothold in England. Surrounded by water, England had built up the greatest navy in the world. Napoléon's navy was no match for England's great ships and skilled sailors.

Napoléon I, considered a savior by some and a monster by others, changed France and the rest of Western Europe forever. He fought to conquer Europe for France, but by the end of his career, France was smaller than when he'd begun. Napoléon was a revolutionary militarist, and he reformed France's educational and financial systems. He also created the Code Napoléon, a compact statement of French law, which served as a model for many Western nations.

France's ships could not defeat the English fleet. But they could hurt England by disrupting the country's sea trade. The English relied on supplies and weapons they imported from other nations. To stop the flow of foreign goods, Napoléon issued several decrees in 1806 and 1807. They ordered all other nations to stop trading with England.

The English government responded with the Orders in Council. These laws were designed to keep France from importing goods it desperately needed. The Orders in Council required all trading ships bound for France to stop in England. Only those licensed by the English government would be allowed to continue on.

The United States refused to take sides in the conflict between France and England. But when it came to their trading restrictions, neither country much cared about America's neutral stance. Unable to trade with France or England, American merchants went bankrupt and American seamen lost their jobs.

Some American traders dared to ignore the restrictions. A few made fortunes conducting illegal trade. But others had their ships seized. Between 1807 and 1812, more than 900 American ships were captured by England, France, and their allies.

Impressment

Many Americans were angered by England's trade restrictions. But they were even more outraged by its policy of impressment. The English often stopped American ships and impressed (forced) English sailors aboard to join the English navy.

While at war with France, England needed every sailor it could find. But the English navy was hard on sailors. They were paid very little and were subjected to harsh discipline. Many English sailors became fed up. About one-fourth of all English sailors abandoned their posts during the Napoleonic Wars. Many found work on American ships, where they could expect much better treatment and pay.

England claimed it had every right to impress these deserters. But the United States said the English had no right to board American ships without permission. The government also claimed that English naval officers sometimes impressed American citizens. Perhaps as many as 6,000 Americans were forced to serve in the English navy against their will.

Impressment infuriated the American public, especially after the *Chesapeake-Leopard* incident. In June 1807, the USS *Chesapeake*, an American ship, was stopped by the HMS *Leopard*, an English vessel. The commander of the *Leopard* demanded the Americans turn over four crew members who had deserted the English navy. The commander of the *Chesapeake* refused. Without warning, the *Leopard* fired on the American ship, killing three and injuring eighteen.

The Embargo

After the *Chesapeake-Leopard* incident, some Americans began calling for war. They wanted to fight England to preserve their nation's honor. President Jefferson knew the military was in no shape to take on such a powerful enemy. He decided instead to establish an embargo. This government order forbade American ships from sailing to any foreign cities.

The embargo was meant to punish England and France, both of which wanted American goods. But the United States ended up suffering the most. American merchants and sailors

The USS *Chesapeake* was a 1244-ton, 36-gun frigate. After much action in the seas, the ship was refitted and sent back out on the waters, where it ran into the HMS *Leopard*. In June 1813, the *Chesapeake* met the British frigate *Shannon* in a violent and unsuccessful battle, shown above. The *Chesapeake* was sold in 1820, and its parts were used for building construction.

lost their livelihood. The embargo also hurt American farmers, especially those in the South. For much of their income, they relied on exporting tobacco, cotton, and rice to England. Under pressure, Jefferson lifted the embargo after fourteen months. In the coming years, the U.S. government tried implementing other trade restrictions, but they generally damaged the American economy more than that of their enemies.

In 1810, the U.S. government tried a new tactic. It passed a law to coax either England or France into lifting its trade restrictions. The law promised that if England agreed first, the United States would cut off all trade with France. But if France agreed

Henry Clay (1777–1852) was an influential player in American politics. He served as senator and Speaker of the House of Representatives most of his life. It was his great eloquence that persuaded Congress to support his desire to go to war with England. He went on to use his talents in negotiations to delay the Civil War for ten years. Clay ran unsuccessfully for the presidency many times and is known for saying, "I would rather be right than be president."

first, all U.S. trade with England would end. Napoléon of France immediately responded. He swore that he would relax his trade rules, and President James Madison took him at his word. Although France continued to interfere with American shipping, Madison cut off all trade with England.

The War Hawks

The tension between the United States and England continued to grow. By late 1811, many Republicans in the U.S. Congress were calling for war. Some thought that if the United States just talked of war, England would back down and lift its restrictions. Others believed war offered the only solution to the nation's problems with England. Among that group were the war hawks. Led by Henry Clay of Kentucky, these young Republicans became the most powerful group in Congress.

The war hawks spoke out against England, accusing the country of violating American shipping rights on the high seas. But they had other reasons for wanting war. The war hawks resented the alliance between the English and several American Indian tribes. They believed the English had encouraged Indians to attack American settlements in the Northwest Territory (now the states of Ohio, Indiana, Illinois, Michigan, Wisconsin, and part of Minnesota).

The war hawks also had an eye on the rich lands of Canada, an area then controlled by England. The war hawks thought the United States could easily conquer Canada. Only about half a million non-Indians lived there, not enough to defend such a large region adequately. Also, many Canadians were of French descent. The war hawks assumed they would not want to fight on the side of the English.

The Federalists Speak Out

Few Federalists shared the Republicans' thirst for war. Many Federalists were from the Northeast. This region relied on trade with England. The people of the Northeast, therefore, had the most to lose if war were declared.

Some Federalists were also suspicious of war plans to invade Canada. They said it was wrong to attack the Canadians when the United States's real gripe was with the English. They also believed it would drive up the cost of the war, since land battles required more troops and supplies than sea battles.

Outnumbered by Republicans by about one to five, the Federalists had little power in Congress. The war hawks ignored their objections and pressed for war. The Republican-led Congress slowly began building up the U.S. Army. However, it refused to raise taxes, preferring instead to borrow money to fund the growing military.

Declaring War

Despite these preparations, most Americans thought the United States would be able to solve its problems with England through negotiation. As one war hawk, William Lowndes, noted in a letter home in March 1812, "We hear from all quarters that people do not expect war." After all, English soldiers were already occupied with fighting Napoléon's troops. Most Americans assumed England would be eager to avoid involvement in a second war.

They were right. As war fever spread in Congress, the English government tried to calm its American enemies. In the spring of 1812, the English navy told its officers to stop interfering with trade along the American coastline. By mid-June, England made an even greater concession: It lifted the Orders in Council. Just a few months before, President Madison had named these hated trade restrictions as England's greatest offense against the United States.

Messengers carrying the news immediately boarded English ships bound for Washington, D.C. But the trip across the Atlantic Ocean took weeks. By the time they arrived, it was too late. Unaware of England's great concession, the U.S. Congress had already declared war.

CHAPTER 2

Republicans across the nation celebrated the declaration of war. But it was soon clear that the United States was far from ready to fight. As the war began, the army had only 7,000 professional soldiers, or regulars. Most were young, inexperienced, and poorly trained. The army's officers were even less prepared for battle. Many were elderly men who had not seen combat since the American Revolution, some thirty years earlier. Others obtained their positions through political connections and had no battlefield experience at all.

ON LAND AND ON SEA

The government tried to recruit more regulars, but few men wanted to join. The army offered low pay, bad food, and inadequate clothing. Unwilling to spend what was needed to improve the regular army, the United States instead decided to rely on militias to fight the war. Militias were armies of ordinary citizens that states called up in times of emergency. Only expected to serve a few months at a time, militiamen generally had little training or equipment.

Luckily for the United States, the English forces in North America were equally unprepared for war. There were about 10,000 English troops in Canada, but they were scattered over a large area. Like the Americans, the English planned for

A Scene on the FRONTIERS as Practiced by the HUMANE BRITISH and their WORTHY ALLIES ___

Bring me the Scalps
and the King our master
will reward you....

Reward for
Sixteen
Scalps

Arise Columbia's Sons and forward press,
Your country's wrongs call loudly for redress;
The Savage Indian with his Scalping knife,
Or Tomahawk, may seek to take your life.

By bravery aw'd they'll in a dreadful Fright,
Shrink back for Refuge to the Woods in Flight;
Their British leaders then will quickly shake,
And for those wrongs shall restitution make.

This political cartoon by William Charles shows an Indian handing over American scalps to a British officer while another Indian adds to the collection. The officer says, "Bring me the scalps and the King our master will reward you," reflecting a story that British Army colonel Henry Proctor purchased American scalps after an Indian massacre. The cartoon was circulated to intensify anti-British feeling in America.

militiamen to do much of the fighting, even though they were unsure of the loyalty of the Canadian militia. Adding to the English forces were warriors from several Indian tribes, including the Winnebago, Menominee, Kickapoo, and Shawnee. These Indian groups had long been trading partners of the English.

The Invasion of Canada

Ready or not, the U.S. Army planned a military invasion of Canada. Engineered by General Henry Dearborn, the plan called for the Americans to attack at three points—at Fort

Henry Dearborn (1751–1829) left his medical practice to fight in the American Revolution. He went on to serve his country as a congressman, secretary of war, and U.S. minister to Portugal. It was the War of 1812 that got the better of his career. As commanding officer of the army's northeast sector, he was responsible for many casualties. Dearborn was removed from command and placed in an administrative position.

Detroit, at the Niagara River, and at Montreal. Most military experts assumed the Americans would score an easy victory. In a letter to journalist William Duane, former President Thomas Jefferson went as far as saying that conquering Canada would be "a mere matter of marching" into the English-held region.

General William Hull, a fifty-nine-year-old veteran of the American Revolution, was chosen to oversee the campaign. On July 5, Hull and about 2,000 soldiers arrived at Fort Detroit (now Detroit, Michigan). From there, they were to cross the Detroit River into Canada and attack Fort Malden (now Amherstburg, Ontario). Soon after starting out, a group of Hull's men were attacked by Indians. Hull panicked and demanded his troops retreat back to Detroit. His soldiers were angry. They began to wonder whether Hull had the courage to lead them into battle.

Also a veteran of the American Revolution, attorney William Hull (1753–1825) was appointed governor of the Michigan Territory by Thomas Jefferson. He became a brigadier general in the War of 1812, which was very nearly the death of him. The man who was known for his courage and confidence fell victim to hesitation and indecision. William Hull's invasion of Canada was so unsuccessful that he was sentenced to death for it. Fortunate enough to be pardoned by President Madison, Hull spent the rest of his life in Massachusetts with his family and never gave up attempts to clear his name.

By intercepting a mailbag of letters, General Isaac Brock, the English commander at Fort Malden, discovered how Hull's men felt about him. The news gave him the confidence to plan an attack of Fort Detroit. First, though, he started a rumor that he had many more Indian soldiers than he actually did. Brock knew Hull was terrified of battling a large Indian force.

Three Forts Lost

By late July, Hull received news that an English and Indian force had taken over Fort Michilimackinac, another American post. In response, he ordered the American soldiers at Fort Dearborn (now Chicago, Illinois) to evacuate. Only fifty-four soldiers were there,

This print shows Captain Nathan Heald in council with the Potawatomi Indians at Fort Dearborn, which was located where the heart of Chicago lies today. Heald was betrayed by the Indians but managed to escape the brutal Fort Dearborn Massacre that left many men, women, and children dead. Instead, he and his wife were taken captive as British prisoners of war by Chief Blackbird.

not enough to defend the fort if the English decided to attack it as well. Nine women and eighteen children were also living there.

On August 15, Captain Nathan Heald led the Americans out of Fort Dearborn. They were escorted by 400 Potawatomi Indians, who promised to protect them. But, about a mile from the fort, the Potawatomi instead turned on the Americans and attacked them. They killed forty and took the rest captive. The Indians burned down the fort and later ransomed most of the captives to the English.

On the same day of the Fort Dearborn attack, the English general Brock and his men surrounded Fort Detroit. As they fired on the fort, Hull stayed in his quarters. Without consulting his officers, he soon sent a white cloth up the fort's flagpole. The general had surrendered Detroit to the English.

Hull's actions stunned his men. They also infuriated his superiors. Hull was later found guilty of treason in a military court and sentenced to death. President Madison, however, pardoned Hull because of his advanced age and his distinguished service in the American Revolution.

More Missteps

After the disaster at Detroit, the U.S. Army readied itself for its next campaign. By the early fall, about 6,000 American soldiers had gathered near the Niagara River. Their commander was Major General Stephen Van Rensselaer. Van Rensselaer planned to take 4,000 of the soldiers across the river and march into Canada. He told General Alexander Smyth to lead the other 2,000 troops in an attack against an English fort as a diversion. But Smyth resented Van Rensselaer's position and refused to follow the order. Although Smyth's disobedience foiled his battle plans, Van Rensselaer led his troops across the Niagara River anyway.

With a limited number of boats, the Americans had to cross the river in shifts. The first groups were fired upon by English soldiers, who hid behind great rocks along the riverbank. They were soon joined by reinforcements led by Isaac Brock. During the battle, Brock was killed by an American sharpshooter.

The Americans were holding their own against the English. Victory seemed within their reach. But when the American

Published in a book by Samuel Lewis in 1813, this map shows the seat of war in North America during the War of 1812. It is housed in the Library of Congress. The waterways dividing the United States and Canada were used strategically during the fighting. In addition, these valuable waters—the Great Lakes and the St. Lawrence River—were part of the reason for the fight.

soldiers waiting to cross the river saw the wounded, many decided to stay where they were. They were largely militiamen whose terms of service did not require them to leave the United States. Van Rensselaer begged the men to cross into Canada, but it was no use. Without the help of the militiamen, the American soldiers lost the battle.

Disgusted, Van Rensselaer resigned his post. The army replaced him with Smyth without realizing that Smyth had lost the support of his men. Smyth made plans to attack Fort Erie on the Niagara, but his own officers refused to follow him. The attack was called off when the militiamen in Smyth's force also refused to cross the U.S. border. The next month, the reluctance of the militia to fight in Canada also ruined the plans for an American invasion of Montreal.

By the end of 1812, the army's dream of an easy victory in Canada was completely dashed. Conquering Canada would be far more than a "mere matter of marching." Success would require good military leaders and loyal, well-trained soldiers— neither of which the American army had. This was the hard-won lesson of a misguided campaign that, as the January 13, 1813, issue of Federalist newspaper *Green-Mountain Farmer* claimed, had brought the United States nothing but "disaster, defeat, disgrace, and ruin and death."

Victory at Sea

If Americans were surprised by their losses in Canada in 1812, they were stunned by their victories on the high seas. As the war began, few saw the U.S. Navy as a threat to England's great fleet. The United States had just seventeen ships, and only seven were frigates (medium-size warships). England, on the other hand, had more than 1,000 ships. Only about 500 were seaworthy at any given time, however, and they were scattered all around the world. Near Canada, there were about thirty-seven English ships, including nine frigates.

In addition to having more ships in North America, the English had by far the more powerful navy. In fact, for more than a hundred years, the English navy had been considered the finest in the world. Although the Americans were clearly the under-dogs, the U.S. Navy was impressive, considering its small size. It boasted many skilled seamen and a few promising young officers, including Stephen Decatur and Oliver Hazard Perry.

The USS *Constitution* sits victoriously in the background while its opponent, the HMS *Guerrière*, explodes into the sea, in this 1812 print by B. Tanner. Included on the print (not shown) are extracts from the *Constitution*'s log, which read, in part: "[R]emov[ed] the prisoners and baggage from the prize to our own ship. Sent a surgeon's mate to assist in attending the wounded . . . [H]aving removed all the prisoners . . . immediately left her on fire, and a quarter past 3, she blew up."

Another young talent was Captain Isaac Hull, the nephew of the disgraced general William Hull. Isaac Hull was placed in command of the USS *Constitution*. It was considered the best of the U.S. Navy's frigates. In early August, the *Constitution* set out from Boston, Massachusetts, and headed south in search of English ships. On August 19, 1812, about 600 miles (966 kilometers) east of the city, the frigate encountered the HMS *Guerrière*, commanded by James R. Decres. The sea battle lasted less than an hour. Hull deftly maneuvered the *Constitution*. Its first shots at the *Guerrière* all but destroyed the great ship. As quoted in Donald R. Hickey's book, *The War of 1812*, an American aboard the *Guerrière* recalled that the shots made a "tremendous explosion," causing the frigate to "reel and tremble as though she had received the shock of an earthquake." The American ship was largely unharmed in the battle. When one sailor claimed he saw a shot bounce off its side, the *Constitution* earned a new nickname: Old Ironsides.

The unexpected victory filled the Americans with pride and the English with panic. The English navy tried to discount the *Guerrière*'s defeat as a fluke. But a string of other American triumphs at sea made that impossible. The most dramatic occurred on October 15.

Commanding the USS *United States*, Captain Stephen Decatur defeated the HMS *Macedonia* in a bloody battle. According to Edgar Stanton Maclay's *History of the United States Navy*, one sailor described the scene when the Americans boarded the English vessel in this way: "[F]ragments of the dead [were] scattered in every direction, the decks [were] slippery with blood, [and there was] one continuous agonizing yell of the unhappy wounded." For capturing the *Macedonia*, Decatur and his crew won a prize of $200,000 from the U.S. government.

The sea victories provided a much-needed boost to American morale after the humiliation of the Canadian campaign. Quoted in Hickey's *The War of 1812*, one officer said, "Our brilliant naval victories serve, in some measure, to wipe out the disgrace brought upon the nation by the conduct of our generals." But as 1812 came to an end, the American forces were still far from victory. On both land and sea, the United States faced a long, hard fight with no end in sight.

CHAPTER 3

As the War of 1812 entered its second year, President James Madison was in an uncomfortable position. He had won reelection in November 1812, but just barely. Many Americans, including members of his own party, began questioning whether Madison was fit to manage the war. The miserable record of American troops in Canada also made some Americans wonder if the United States should be fighting England at all.

But just as the public was losing confidence, the U.S. military began taking dramatic steps to improve its fighting force. Congress authorized higher pay for soldiers to attract new recruits. By the spring of 1813, there were about 30,000 men in uniform. The government also approved the building of new ships. Perhaps most important of all, the president appointed a new secretary of war, John Armstrong. Under Armstrong, the army was run more efficiently. Many of the older leaders were replaced by promising young officers, such as William Henry Harrison and Andrew Jackson.

VICTORY AND DEFEAT

The Sack of York

When the spring came, the U.S. Army made plans for a new Canadian campaign. Its goal was to gain control of Lake Ontario and Lake Erie. These lakes provided the best water route for

John Armstrong (1758–1843) fought in the American Revolution before serving in the U.S. Congress and U.S. Senate. During the Revolution he wrote the Newburgh Address, attacking congress. As secretary of war during the War of 1812, Armstrong made some poor decisions. One striking example was when he assured President Madison that it was safe to remain in Washington, D.C., as the British approached Maryland. Armstrong also angered many by neglecting to follow the chain of command. Still, he made his mark on history by overseeing the "Rules and Regulations of the Army of the United States," which is still used today.

moving men and supplies into Canada. Whoever controlled these lakes would control the region.

Captain Isaac Chauncey was chosen to head the operations on the lakes. Chauncey worked hard to build up the American fleet by buying merchant vessels and converting them into war ships. He also established a naval base at Presque Isle off Lake Erie. The United States already had a base on Lake Ontario at Sackets Harbor, New York.

Chauncey's first mission was to attack the town of York (now Toronto, Ontario) on Lake Ontario. York was the capital of Upper Canada. In April 1813, an American force of 1,700 left Sackets Harbor. It was commanded by General Zebulon Pike,

General Zebulon Pike (1779–1813) was an explorer for the U.S. Army, during which time he led many expeditions and negotiated Indian treaties. He lost his life in the War of 1812 attack on York, which his men avenged by destroying the town of York. This led the British to conduct a perhaps even more serious attack. Before the battle in York, Pike wrote a letter to his father which read, "If we go into Canada, you will hear of my fame or of my death—for I am determined to seek the 'Bubble' even in the cannon's mouth."

who had already gained fame as an explorer. Pike and his soldiers rushed into York while a fleet of warships under Chauncey's command fired on the town. With only 700 English soldiers to protect it, York was quickly captured.

The Americans, however, suffered high causalities. During the battle, the English blew up a store of ammunition so it would not fall into enemy hands. Several hundred U.S. soldiers, including Pike, died in the explosion. The grisly scene filled the survivors with fury. Once the English had surrendered, the Americans sought revenge by running through York, stealing property and destroying buildings. The English were appalled by the sacking of York and vowed revenge.

The fighting on Lake Ontario continued into the summer. In May, an American force won control of Fort George. This important post was located on the Niagara, the river that connected Lake Ontario and Lake Erie. The victory was short-lived, though. By the winter of 1813, only 250 cold and tired soldiers were assigned to protect the fort. In December, the English easily took over not only Fort George, but also the nearby Fort Niagara. They managed to hold control of these forts and the Niagara River until the end of the war.

Meeting the Enemy

The American force had better luck in the battle for Lake Erie. Chauncey placed Commodore Oliver Hazard Perry in charge of the American operation there. The talented twenty-seven-year-old officer scrambled for months to build and repair ships and search for sailors to fill out his crews. By mid-August, Perry had nine ships. He was ready to face the English.

The English force on Lake Erie was commanded by Captain Robert H. Barclay. An experienced officer, Barclay had lost an arm while fighting against Napoléon's forces. Although the English had only six ships, he decided to strike first. On September 10, the battle began. Nearly all the ships were damaged. Perry's ship, the USS *Lawrence*, was left in ruins. About 80 percent of its crew was killed or wounded.

Still, Perry refused to surrender. With four sailors, he boarded a small boat and rowed toward the USS *Niagara*, an American frigate that had stayed back during the battle. Amid pounding enemy fire, Perry made it to the *Niagara*, took over the ship, and continued the fight.

The English were soon overwhelmed. In the three-hour battle, all of the largest English ships were destroyed. Most of their officers

Born in 1785, Oliver Hazard Perry served a long and distinguished military career for the United States. His victory on Lake Erie during the War of 1812 earned him the rank of captain and a vote of thanks from Congress. In 1819, Perry died from yellow fever in Port of Spain, Trinidad, on a return trip from South America.

were dead or wounded. Barclay, whose good arm was mangled during the battle, was among the casualties. The English reluctantly surrendered, giving the U.S. Navy its greatest victory of the war. Hailed for his coolness in the heat of battle, Perry became a national hero. A phrase he wrote in a letter to William Henry Harrison became famous: "We have met the enemy and they are ours."

Battle of the Thames

Perry's victory on Lake Erie spelled disaster for an English force led by General Henry Proctor. During the summer of 1813,

The Battle of the Thames was a crushing defeat for the British. And with Tecumseh's death, his Indian followers broke their alliance with the British and lost power in their territories. The victory brought fame to American general William Henry Harrison, who had previously worked to strengthen the force of white settlers in Indian territories by obtaining the titles to native lands. Harrison became the ninth president of the United States, although he died of pneumonia his first month in office.

Proctor's force had staged several unsuccessful attacks on American forts on the lake's western shores. But once the Americans took control of Lake Erie, Proctor had little choice but to give up his campaign. The Americans would not allow any English supply ships to reach them.

Proctor's decision infuriated the Indian leader Tecumseh. Proctor's army was made up of 900 regulars and 1,200 Indians recruited by Tecumseh. He and his warriors supported the

English because they despised Americans for taking over Indian land. In Tecumseh's eyes, Proctor's retreat was a betrayal. In *Niles Register*, a Baltimore newspaper, Tecumseh called the English officer a coward, comparing him to "a fat animal" that "drops [its tail] between its legs and runs off" when frightened.

Under pressure from Tecumseh, Proctor agreed to make one last stand. As his English troops withdrew, they were chased by a 5,500-man American force led by General William Henry Harrison. On October 5, Proctor and his men turned around and faced them in battle at Moraviantown on the Thames River. The large American force quickly surrounded them. Tired and hungry, the English troops surrendered. The Indian force, however, continued to fight until it heard that the great Tecumseh had been killed. Devastated by the news, they gave up the fight as well. The American victory was not only the war's last significant battle in the Northwest Territory, it also marked the end of organized Indian resistance to American settlement in the region.

The Naval War

During 1813, the American army had redeemed itself. Perry's triumph on Lake Erie and Harrison's victory at the Battle of the Thames especially restored American confidence in the land war. On the sea, however, they suffered a series of disappointments.

The previous year, the English had underestimated the American navy. Vowing not to make the same mistake again, they sent nearly 100 ships to American waters. By November 1813, the English navy had formed a blockade—a wall of ships that prevented American vessels from moving freely. The blockade stretched along most of the Atlantic coast, from Florida to southern New England. Because some northeastern merchants

The British blockade of the East Coast devastated the United States and ruined its commerce and military strategy. England's hold on the coastline allowed it to attack docks and harbors, chipping away at the defense in American port cities. The 1813 watercolor shown above, painted by artist William Paine, shows the blockade of New England, which was lighter than coverage on the rest of the coast.

were willing to trade with the English, much of the New England coastline was left undisturbed.

The blockade had a devastating effect on the U.S. economy. Merchants could no longer export American goods to Europe or import European goods to America. The end of free trade also meant that in many regions of the United States, certain products were in short supply. With shortages came high prices. In some areas, the price of items such as sugar, salt, tea, and cotton skyrocketed.

Attacking the Coast

The blockade did more than disrupt trade. It also crippled the U.S. Navy. Few American warships were able to leave port to engage the English in battle. The Americans and English had only four naval duels in 1813. The United States lost three.

Once in control of U.S. waters, the English began a new campaign of harassing American coastal cities. In April, English soldiers attacked Frenchtown, Maryland. For the next twelve days, they raided other Maryland towns, destroying homes and terrorizing the people who lived there.

The next month, English forces launched an even more brutal attack on Hampton, Virginia. Charles Napier, a young English officer, was appalled by the violence. He wrote in his journal that "every horror was committed with impunity: rape, murder, pillage; and not a man was punished!"

The English invasion into U.S. soil was designed to make Americans lose faith in the war. But the worst was yet to come. The next year would see the most devastating attack of the war, with the U.S. capital of Washington, D.C., as its target.

CHAPTER 4

On December 30, 1813, an English ship sailed into American waters. It did not come to fight but to make peace. Aboard was a message to the U.S. government: England was ready to enter peace negotiations. Madison assembled a team of commissioners and sent them to Ghent, Belgium, where they would meet with English negotiators.

INVADING WASHINGTON

For the United States, the movement toward peace came hardly a minute too soon. Just two months earlier, the English and their European allies had defeated the French emperor Napoléon at the Battle of Leipzig. The English victory meant that the Napoleonic Wars would soon be over. The English would then be able to send more soldiers to North America to fight. Many American officials worried that the U.S. military would be overwhelmed by a bigger and better English force.

The diagram on the right shows the positioning of American troops at Horseshoe Bend. It was drawn in 1814 by R. H. McEwen, an officer who fought in the battle. The Battle at Horseshoe Bend was the last battle of the Creek or Red Stick War of 1813–1814, which is considered part of the War of 1812. The result was that many Creek Indians fled to Florida. Several Creek leaders who remained signed the Treaty of Fort Jackson, which forfeited much of their land to the United States.

Being great Marks to a Regiment, Inasmuch
entitles to carry a Sword, this I arrived to do I went
to fight, I therefore carried a large rifle the whole rout,

R.H. McEwen

Town

Low Grounds

High Grounds

2

Tallipoosa River   Breast work   Islands   Ferry

Regular   Militia

When this desertion of the head spread thro' the
encampment, On my had the morning after the battle,
that is the encampment about 10 o'clock R.H. McEwen about noon
clean — I was a Regiment the guards under to a Regiment of Indians
two from East Tennessee Commanded by Col. John Brown, we
Col. Covington & Co. the 23d July 1814 for the Cuba station returned to the fort. This
highlights it Maj the committee [...] him prisoners. R.H. McEwen

Figure 1 Represents the Breast Works

Figure 2 the Sally part which was a small avenue
through which a man could just pass

The line marked thus ‖‖‖‖ represents the 39th Reg.
Militia and Artillery Charging the Works.

eeeee This Represents the Mounted Gun men on the opposite
side of the river from the fort.

R. H. McEwen

This Battle fought on Sunday the 27th March 1814. 557 enemy counted
dead on the ground. 125 of our men fell. 106 wounded some Mortally —
Its supposed number more at the river & fell. but [...] drowned into the river & not found.

37

Horseshoe Bend

The first fighting of 1814 did not pit the United States against the English. Instead, the enemy was a faction of the Creek Indians. The Creeks were a large tribe whose territory stretched over much of present-day Alabama and Georgia. One group of Creeks known as the Red Sticks was tired of Americans invading their land. The Red Sticks were willing to go to war to keep Americans out of their territory. After several skirmishes with Americans, on August 30, 1813, the Red Sticks attacked Fort Mims, a post in what is now Alabama. Creek warriors killed about 250 people at the fort, including many women and children. The news of the massacre spread terror among the American settlers in the region.

Several states sent out their militias to punish the Creeks. The most enthusiastic militiamen were from Tennessee. They were commanded by Major General Andrew Jackson. His troops launched successful attacks on the Creek towns of Tallushatchee and Talladega before disbanding for the winter. But by early 1814, Jackson had reassembled a 4,000-man army and was again ready to fight.

In March, Jackson learned that a group of Red Stick Creeks were at Horseshoe Bend in present-day Alabama. The Indians' camp was on a peninsula that jutted into the Tallapoosa River. In case they needed to make a quick getaway, the Creeks left their canoes along the riverbank. Jackson sent some Indians in his fighting force to steal the canoes. Then he positioned some troops at the front of the Indian camp and some at the rear. On March 27, they attacked. The fighting was bloody. Though surrounded, many of the Red Stick Creeks were determined to fight to the death. More than 800 died, including some women and children. Soundly defeated by Jackson's soldiers, most of the survivors fled to Florida, an area then controlled by Spain.

With the American victory at Horseshoe Bend, the Creek War came to an end. Now a war hero, Jackson compelled the tribe to sign a punishing peace treaty. Even though many Creeks were friendly to Americans and had helped them defeat the Red Stick Creeks, the tribe was forced to give up 20 million acres of land—about half its territory—to the United States.

The Chesapeake Campaign

By July 1814, American troops were again battling the English. The major land campaign was fought along the Niagara River. At the Battle of the Chippewa and the Battle of Lundy's Lane, the Americans surprised well-trained English soldiers with their discipline and determination. Even English veterans of the brutal Napoleonic Wars claimed the fighting was the most intense they had ever seen. In August, the English were equally impressed by the New York militia during an attack on Lake Erie. Several months later, another English squadron experienced an unexpected defeat to the east at Lake Champlain. News of these battles filled Americans with pride. Finally, their spirited soldiers had proven they could hold their own against the more experienced English fighting forces.

In late 1814, the English met with far more success in their naval campaign along the Atlantic coast. They focused on attacking towns along the Chesapeake Bay, a body of water that borders Virginia and Maryland. The Chesapeake coast offered the English two particularly enticing targets—the cities of Baltimore and Washington, D.C.

Baltimore was a center of shipbuilding. And since the Baltimore Riots of 1812, the city was also a well-known hotbed for anti-English feelings. A successful attack on the city, therefore, would be doubly sweet for the English. Not only would it allow them to destroy a large number of American ships, but it would also give them a chance to punish many of their most vocal American critics.

The English interest in attacking Washington, D.C., was more emotional than practical. There was no strategic advantage in taking over the city. It had no military targets, like the shipbuilding yards of Baltimore. But as the U.S. capital, it had symbolic importance. An attack on Washington, D.C., would be the ultimate insult to England's American enemies and perfect revenge for the sack of York.

The Blandensburg Races

American officials were slow to recognize the threat to Washington. Secretary of War John Armstrong did not think the English would bother attacking the capital. He assigned only about 500 army regulars to protect the city.

But by mid-August 1814, even Armstrong could see what the English planned to do. On August 18, officials in Washington learned that about 4,500 English soldiers had landed at Benedict, Maryland, and were ready to march toward the capital. The U.S. government frantically called for help from the Maryland and Pennsylvania militia. Within days, some 7,000 militiamen descended on the city.

On the afternoon of August 24, the two forces met at the town of Blandensburg, Maryland. The hastily gathered militia proved no match for the well-trained English army. Almost as

This British political cartoon shows President James Madison and another man, probably Secretary of War John Armstrong, fleeing a blazing Washington, D.C. The caption below the cartoon reads, "The fall of Washington—or Maddy in full flight." The cartoon reveals the lack of respect England had for the United States. Madison's cabinet members are drawn as buffoons, speaking lines such as "The great Washington fought for liberty, but we are fighting for shadows, which if obtained can do us no earthly good but this is the blessed effects of it."

soon as the battle started, the Americans began to retreat. Many ran so fast that the English later jokingly called the battle the "Blandensburg races." By four o'clock, the English had scored a resounding victory.

Washington Ablaze

News of the defeat at Blandensburg soon reached Washington. With no American force to protect them, most people fled the

THE TAKING OF THE CITY OF WASHINGTON IN AMERICA

The Taking of the City of Washington in America was published by G. Thompson in 1814, most likely in London, where such a scene would be met with delight. The work depicts Washington, D.C., ablaze and under siege by British forces, as seen from the Potomac River. Although attacking Washington earned England no significant strategic victory, it did serve to avenge the brutal sacking of York by hitting the heart of the United States.

city in panic. Even President Madison left the capital, escaping by horse-drawn carriage to Virginia. Before fleeing, his wife, Dolley, loaded up a wagon full of important government documents, leaving most of her personal belongings behind.

At about eight o'clock in the evening, the English soldiers reached Washington. Their commander, Robert Ross, searched for someone to negotiate the city's surrender, but all U.S. officials were gone. Ross then ordered his troops to destroy several public buildings. They set ablaze the Capitol, where Congress met, and the buildings that housed the War Department, Treasury Department, and the Library of Congress.

English soldiers also invaded the White House, where the president's table was set for dinner. As one officer, Lieutenant-General Sir Harry Smith, later recounted in his autobiography, "We found a supper all ready, which many of us speedily consumed . . . and drank some very good wine also." Once they finished their meal, they set fire to the building.

With the fires still smoldering, the English left Washington the next morning. Two days later, on August 27, Madison returned. The people of Washington gave him a cool welcome. Many blamed the president for failing to make adequate preparations before the attack. According to *The Dawn's Early Light*, a book by Walter Lord, one angry Washingtonian scrawled on a wall, "George Washington founded this city after a seven years' war with England—James Madison lost it after a two years' war."

The Battle of Baltimore

Meanwhile, the English troops headed toward their next target—Baltimore. The people there had heard about what happened in

Washington. They were determined to make sure that their city would not meet the same fate.

Baltimore had already done a great deal to protect itself from invasion. Samuel Smith, a Maryland senator, had called up the state's militia. He organized every able-bodied man in Baltimore to help build walls made of earth around the city.

On September 12, English ships carrying Ross's 4,500-man army landed fourteen miles (22.5 km) from Baltimore. As they began marching toward the city, they met Maryland militiamen, ready and eager for battle. One American sharpshooter shot and killed Ross—a loss that devastated the morale of the English troops.

Things only got worse for the English. As their army approached Baltimore, they were stunned to find the city so well fortified. Colonel Arthur Brooke, who took command after Ross's death, decided a land invasion was too risky and withdrew his troops.

The English instead attacked by sea. On the night of September 13, English ships began bombarding Fort McHenry, which defended Baltimore's harbor. For twenty-four hours straight, the English ships fired more than 1,500 rounds of ammunition. Only a fraction hit the fort, however. Before the battle, clever American officers had sunk more than twenty ships in the harbor, creating an underwater wall. Unable to get close enough to do much damage, the English gave up. Through their hard work and quick thinking, the people of Baltimore had saved their city.

"The Star-Spangled Banner"

While the English bombarded Fort McHenry, Francis Scott Key, a young American lawyer and amateur poet, watched and

The Star-Spangled banner.

O! say, can you see by the dawn's early light
What so proudly we hail'd by the twilight's last gleaming?
Whose bright stars & broad stripes, through the clouds of the fight
O'er the ramparts we watch'd were so gallantly streaming?
And the rocket's red glare, the bombs bursting in air
Gave proof through the night that our flag was still there
O! say does that star-spangled banner yet wave
O'er the land of the free & the home of the brave?

On that shore, dimly seen through the mists of the deep,
Where the foe's haughty host in dread silence reposes,
What is that which the breeze, o'er the towering steep,
As it fitfully blows, half conceals, half discloses?
Now it catches the gleam of the morning's first beam,
In full glory reflected, now shines on the stream.
'Tis the star-spangled banner — O long may it wave
O'er the land of the free & the home of the brave.

And where is that host that so vauntingly swore
That the havoc of war & the battle's confusion
A home & a country should leave us no more?
Their blood has wash'd out their foul footstep's pollution.
No refuge could save the hireling & slave
From the terror of flight or the gloom of the grave,
And the star-spangled banner in triumph doth wave
O'er the land of the free & the home of the brave.

O! thus be it ever when freemen shall stand
Between their lov'd homes & the war's desolation.
Blest with vict'ry & peace, may the heav'n rescued land
Praise the power that hath made & preserv'd us a nation.
Then conquer we must when our cause it is just,
And this be our motto — In God is our trust,
And the star-spangled banner in triumph shall wave
O'er the land of the free and the home of the brave.

Washington
Oct 21 — 40.   F S Key

waited. He was on a small boat, tethered to an English warship. The English aboard had taken a friend of his captive, and Key had come to his rescue. The English agreed to let his friend go, but would not allow the two Americans to leave until after the battle was over.

Fort McHenry stood eight miles (13 km) away. Above it flew an enormous American flag. As the battle began after dawn, Key watched the exploding bombs light up the fort and flag. But by afternoon, the sky was so dark with rain, Key no longer could see what was happening.

Finally, the next morning, the sky cleared. Through the haze, Key spied the great flag flying high above Fort McHenry. Thrilled that the Americans had won, he began writing a poem called "The Defence of Fort McHenry." Two months later, it was printed as sheet music, set to an old English tune. Retitled "The Star-Spangled Banner," the words and music quickly became one of America's favorite patriotic songs. In 1931, it was named the national anthem of the United States.

CHAPTER 5

AT PEACE

While Washington and Baltimore were under attack, representatives of England and America met to discuss the terms of peace. After months of delay, the peace negotiators gathered in Ghent, Belgium, in early August 1814. President Madison sent a five-member commission that included John Quincy Adams and Henry Clay. The American negotiators were prepared to compromise.

The English commissioners, however, were less flexible. They made several demands the Americans thought were unreasonable. Among them was a proposal to turn the Northwest Territory into a reservation for England's North American Indian allies. The American negotiators refused. About 100,000 non-Indian Americans lived on this land. They knew the U.S. government would not force these people to abandon their homes.

The negotiations seemed hopelessly stalled. But when the American force successfully defended Baltimore, the English negotiators began to rethink their position. On the battlefront, neither side was emerging as the clear winner. It seemed as if the war would go on forever, unless the English commissioners were truly willing to negotiate. With the English tired of war, they finally agreed to work out a peace both sides could live with.

The Hartford Convention or *LEAP NO LEAP.*

This political cartoon, entitled "The Hartford Convention or Leap No Leap," was created by William Charles. It is clear the artist disapproves of the meeting, as he depicts some New England states as cowards seceding and jumping into the arms of England. British king George III is shown at right, encouraging the states of Rhode Island, Connecticut, and Massachusetts to leap off a cliff. In the lower left corner is a medal bearing the names of American heroes from the War of 1812, such as Perry and Hull. The medal's ribbon reads, "This is the produce of the land they wish to abandon."

The Hartford Convention

In late 1814, many Americans were also clamoring for an end to the war. The most vocal continued to be the Federalist politicians of New England. To discuss their opposition to the war, Federalist leaders from five states came together in Hartford, Connecticut, on December 15.

After three weeks of meetings, they issued a report. It called for adding seven amendments to the U.S. Constitution. Among them was an amendment to limit presidents to one term in office. It was a clear signal of their disapproval of how the Republican president James Madison had managed the war during his second term.

The Federalists hoped the Hartford Convention would increase support for their party. But the strategy backfired. The Federalists wanted to be seen as wise and caring leaders, determined to guide the nation toward peace. Instead, the press and the public branded them as traitors, recklessly criticizing their country in its hour of need.

The Battle of New Orleans

While politicians were debating the merits of the war, the fighting continued. The heaviest action was along the coast of the Gulf of Mexico. In the final months of 1814, the English were preparing for an invasion of the gulf coast. Their ultimate target was New Orleans, Louisiana. New Orleans was the largest city in the American South. Located at the mouth of the Mississippi River, it was also an important center for trade. Blockaded by the English, ships filled with millions of dollars worth of merchandise rested in its port. If the English took over the city, they could help themselves to this valuable cargo.

After his dramatic victory at Horseshoe Bend, Andrew Jackson was placed in charge of the U.S. Army in the South. He rushed to prepare New Orleans for invasion. Jackson sent thousands of regular soldiers and militiamen to work building up the city's defenses. He also sought out additional recruits to strengthen his fighting force. Jackson invited Choctaw Indian warriors, free African Americans, and even local pirates to join the battle.

After three brief skirmishes, the English were ready for a full-scale invasion on January 8, 1815. A few hours after dawn, their 5,300-man force marched toward the city. The Americans fired

This print depicting the Battle of New Orleans shows Andrew Jackson at the center, below a U.S. flag, his sword raised to the sky. The American victory at New Orleans made Jackson a national hero. A congressman from Georgia commended him for "illustrating the patriotic defence of the country with brilliant achievement, and signalizing the Americans by steady perseverence, incessant vigilance, patient suffering, undaunted firmness, and in victory moderation and clemency." Jackson went on to become the United States's seventh president.

cannons, rifles, and muskets at the approaching enemy. At first, the invaders were hard to see in the early-morning fog. But as the fog lifted, the Americans were able to mow down the lines of English soldiers. Their leader, Major General Edward Pakenham, was killed by a cannonball as he rallied his frightened troops to continue the fight. Taking command of the English force, General John Lamb realized the situation was hopeless. He ordered his soldiers to retreat.

The Battle of New Orleans was one of the greatest defeats of English military history. The English lost about 2,000 men, while only about 70 Americans were killed. The astounding victory was celebrated across the United States.

The Treaty of Ghent

Americans soon had another reason to cheer. On February 11, 1815, the English ship HMS *Favorite* arrived in New York City. On board was Henry Carroll, Henry Clay's secretary. He carried a copy of the Treaty of Ghent. It had been signed by the peace commissioners of the United States and England on December 24, 1814. The war would not officially end, however, until the treaty was ratified, or approved, by the governments of both nations.

Word of the treaty quickly spread. New Yorkers took to the streets to celebrate. The city was full of the sounds of bells ringing and guns firing into the air. On horseback, messengers carried the news to other cities. Soon, all of the country was hailing the end of the war.

Madison made a special announcement to Congress. He declared that the war was an event "highly honorable to the nation," distinguished "by the most brilliant successes." The president did his best to present the war's end as an American victory.

The Treaty of Ghent, however, told a different story. The document called for nothing more than a return to the situation before the war began. Two issues Madison had named as the primary causes of the war—the English Orders in Council and the impressment of soldiers—were not even mentioned in the treaty.

Costs and Casualties

Even if the treaty changed little, the war itself had an important impact on American society and politics. The cost of the war alone had taken a huge toll on the U.S. government. The United States was nearly bankrupt after spending $158 million to build up the American military. Many citizens, especially those who

Treaty of

Peace and Amity

between

His Britannic Majesty

and

The United States of America

His Britannic Majesty and the United States of America desirous of terminating the War which has unhappily subsisted between the two Countries and of restoring upon principles of perfect reciprocity, Peace, Friendship, and good Understanding between them, have for that purpose appointed their respective Plenipotentiaries, that is to say, His Britannic Majesty on his part has appointed the Right Honourable James Lord Gambier, late Admiral of the White now Admiral of the Red Squadron

The Treaty of Ghent was signed and sealed by many notable men, including Henry Clay and John Quincy Adams. See transcript excerpt on page 57. Although the treaty signaled the end of the War of 1812, it did nothing to solve the issues that had brought about the war in the first place. Still, the United States came away from the experience with a greater sense of independence and national pride, as well as confidence in its military and power over many Indian tribes and their lands.

worked in the shipping industry, had also suffered financial setbacks because of the war.

The cost in human lives was even more alarming. The battle casualties were relatively low. Only about 2,300 American soldiers were killed. Approximately 4,500 more were wounded. However, some 17,000 Americans died of other, nonbattle-related causes. Many fell victim to disease. Unsanitary military camps had caused the rapid spread of typhoid, pneumonia, malaria, dysentery, measles, and smallpox from soldier to soldier.

The war also exposed several weaknesses in the American government. Early in the fighting, it was clear the U.S. military was not up to defending the country. Its officers were old and incompetent, and it had far too few regular soldiers to wage an effective war. As the conflict continued, the government had to scramble to create an adequate fighting force.

The War of 1812 showed weaknesses, as well, in President Madison's leadership. He was often too cautious to manage the war well. Madison was also unable to stop infighting among congressmen or inspire much confidence in the American people. As Senator Henry Clay wrote in a December 29, 1812, letter to politician Caesar A. Rodney, "Mr. Madison is wholly unfit for the storms of war."

Yet, once the country was at peace, most Americans forgot Madison's mishandling of the war. They were far less willing to excuse the Federalists for their antiwar stance, however. As the Treaty of Ghent proved, the Federalists had been right all along—going to war with England accomplished little but had cost a great deal. But instead of praising the Federalists for their foresight, the public condemned them as unpatriotic. Within a few years, the Federalist Party had all but disappeared from American politics.

How the War Changed America

In some ways, the War of 1812 changed the United States for the better. The problems with the military, for instance, taught the government a valuable lesson. After the war, it strove to keep a peacetime army of at least 10,000 soldiers. The military also finally realized the value in encouraging and training talented young officers. Many would play vital roles in later conflicts, including the Mexican-American War (1846–1848).

The war also helped boost the political careers of several men who were later elected president. James Monroe served as secretary of state during the war, while John Quincy Adams distinguished himself as the leader of the American peace commissioners. Two young military heroes—Andrew Jackson and William Henry Harrison—would also draw on their war records to win the presidency.

Non-Indian Americans in the Northwest Territory certainly benefited from the war. The Indians there had fought long and hard to keep their land. But their resistance ended with the defeat of Tecumseh's warriors at the Battle of the Thames in 1813. Now Americans rushed into the Northwest Territory, beginning a westward movement of settlers that would continue for much of the nineteenth century.

Perhaps most important, the War of 1812 gave the United States a new sense of confidence. The war had been a draw. But most Americans remembered it as a victory, largely because they learned of the peace treaty just after they heard of the American triumph at the Battle of New Orleans. In fact, the peace treaty had had nothing to with the outcome of the battle; it had been signed more than a week before the battle had even been fought. Still, Americans welcomed the illusion that the English

Kerchiefs such as this were manufactured as souvenirs following the War of 1812. Printed on the cotton scarf are various scenes of battle in which the United States was victorious. Such a keepsake would help boost the morale of the United States, as national sentiment swelled with each military victory, especially toward the end of the war.

had agreed to end the war only after U.S. forces had beaten the powerful English military. The belief united the country. The War of 1812 may have been a pointless and costly struggle. But Americans chose to recall it as a glorious moment—one that filled them with pride and hope for their young nation.

PRIMARY SOURCE TRANSCRIPTIONS

Page 45: The Star-Spangled Banner

TRANSCRIPTION

The Star-Spangled Banner
O! Say, can you see by the dawn's early light
What so proudly we hail'd by the twilight's last gleaming
Whose bright stars and broad stripes, through the clouds of the fight,
O'er the ramparts we watched were so gallantly streaming?
And the rocket's red glare, the bombs bursting in air
Gave proof through the night that our flag was still there.
O say does that star spangled banner yet wave
O'er the land of the free and the home of the brave?

On that shore dimly seen throughout the mists of the deep
Where the foe's haughty host in dread silence reposes
What is that which the breeze o'er the towering steep
As it fitfully blows, half conceals, half discloses?
Now it catches the gleam of the morning's first beam
In full glory reflected now shines on the stream.
'Tis the Star-Spangled Banner, Oh long may it wave
O'er the land of the free and the home of the brave.

And where is that band who so hauntingly swore
That the havoc of war and the battle's confusion
A home and country, shall leave us no more?
Their blood was washed out their foul foot steps pollution
No refuge could save the hireling and slave
From the terror of flight or the gloom of the grave.
And the Star-Spangled Banner in triumph doth wave
O'er the land of the free and the home of the brave.

Oh thus be it e'er when free men shall stand
Between their lov'd homes and war's desolation!
Blest with vict'ry and peace, may the heav'n rescued land
Praise the Pow'r that has made and presrv'd us a nation
And conquer we must when our cause is just
And this be our motto: "In God is our trust."
And the Star-Spangled Banner in triumph shall wave
O'er the land of the free and the home of the brave.
Washington   F. S. Key
Oct 21 –40

Page 52: Treaty of Ghent

TRANSCRIPTION EXCERPT

Treaty of Peace and Amity between His Britannic Majesty and the United States of America...

There shall be a firm and universal Peace between His Britannic Majesty and the United States, and between their respective Countries, Territories, Cities, Towns, and People of every degree without exception of places or persons. All hostilities both by sea and land shall cease as soon as this Treaty shall have been ratified by both parties as hereinafter mentioned...

The United States of America engage to put an end immediately after the Ratification of the present Treaty to hostilities with all the Tribes or Nations of Indians with whom they may be at war at the time of such Ratification, and forthwith to restore to such Tribes or Nations respectively all the possessions, rights, and privileges which they may have enjoyed or been entitled to in one thousand eight hundred and eleven previous to such hostilities. Provided always that such Tribes or Nations shall agree to desist from all hostilities against the United States of America, their Citizens, and Subjects upon the Ratification of the present Treaty being notified to such Tribes or Nations, and shall so desist accordingly...

This Treaty when the same shall have been ratified on both sides without alteration by either of the contracting parties, and the Ratifications mutually exchanged, shall be binding on both parties, and the Ratifications shall be exchanged at Washington in the space of four months from this day or sooner if practicable. In faith whereof, We the respective Plenipotentiaries have signed this Treaty, and have hereunto affixed our Seals.

Done in triplicate at Ghent the twenty fourth day of December one thousand eight hundred and fourteen.

GAMBIER. [Seal]

HENRY GOULBURN [Seal]

WILLIAM ADAMS [Seal]

JOHN QUINCY ADAMS [Seal]

J. A. BAYARD [Seal]

H. CLAY. [Seal]

JON. RUSSELL [Seal]

ALBERT GALLATIN [Seal]

GLOSSARY

blockade A group of ships used to prevent other ships from entering or leaving an area.

campaign A series of military operations aimed at a specific purpose.

commerce The buying and selling of goods.

embargo A government order prohibiting trade with another nation.

export To send goods to another country for sale.

frigate A fast, medium-sized warship used in the nineteenth century.

import To bring in goods from another country for sale.

impressment Seizing men to serve as sailors or soldiers.

merchant A person who buys and sells goods for profit.

militia A military force made up of ordinary citizens rather than professional soldiers.

morale A feeling of confidence and enthusiasm.

neutral Supporting neither side in a war.

political party Political group organized to promote certain policies and candidates for public office.

port A coastal town or city where ships load and unload goods.

regular A professional soldier in a nation's permanent standing army.

retreat To withdraw soldiers from a battlefield.

sack To rob and destroy a captured city or town.

# FOR MORE INFORMATION

Battlefield House Museum
77 King Street West
P.O. Box 66561
Stoney Creek, ON L8G 5E5
Canada
(905) 662-8458
Web site: http://www.battlefieldhouse.ca

Fort McHenry National Monument and Historic Shrine
End of East Fort Avenue
Baltimore, MD 21230
(410) 962-4290
Web site: http://www.nps.gov/fomc

Web Sites

Due to the changing nature of Internet links, the Rosen Publishing Group, Inc., has developed an online list of Web sites related to the subject of this book. This site is updated regularly. Please use this link to access the list:

http://www.rosenlinks.com/psah/ware

# FOR FURTHER READING

Berton, Pierre. *Attack on Montreal: The Battles of the War of 1812*. Toronto: McClelland & Stewart, 1996.

Livesey, Robert. *The Defenders*. Toronto: Stoddart Kids, 1999.

Shorto, Russell. *Tecumseh and the Dream of an American Indian Nation*. Englewood Cliffs, NJ: Silver Burnett Press, 1989.

Smolinski, Diane, and Henry Smolinski. *Soldiers of the War of 1812*. Chicago: Heinemann Library, 2002.

Stefoff, Rebecca. *The War of 1812*. New York: Benchmark Books, 2001.

Taylor, Lonn. *The Star-Spangled Banner: The Flag That Inspired the National Anthem*. New York: Harry N. Abrams, 2000.

Warrick, Karen Clemens. *The War of 1812: "We Have Met the Enemy and They Are Ours."* Berkeley Heights, NJ: Enslow Publishers, 2002.

# BIBLIOGRAPHY

Chambers, John Whiteclay II, ed. *The Oxford Companion to American Military History*. New York: Oxford University Press, 1999.

Elting, John R. *Amateurs, to Arms!: A Military History of the War of 1812*. New York: Da Capo Press, 1995.

Heidler, David Stephen, and Jeanne T. Heidler, eds. *Encyclopedia of the War of 1812*. Santa Barbara, CA: ABC-CLIO, 1997.

Hickey, Donald R. *The War of 1812: A Forgotten Conflict*. Urbana, IL: University of Illinois Press, 1990.

Hickey, Donald R. *The War of 1812: A Short History*. Urbana, IL: University of Illinois Press, 1995.

Howes, Kelly King. *The War of 1812*. Detroit: UXL, 2002.

Taylor, Lonn. *The Star-Spangled Banner: The Flag that Inspired the National Anthem*. New York: Harry N. Abrams, 2000.

PRIMARY SOURCE IMAGE LIST

INDEX

About the Author

Liz Sonneborn is a writer and an editor living in Brooklyn, New York. A graduate of Swarthmore College, she has written more than thirty books for children and adults, including *The American West*, *A to Z of American Women in the Performing Arts*, and *The New York Public Library's Amazing Native American History*, winner of a 2000 Parent's Choice Award.

Photo Credits

Cover, pp. 1, 13, 25, 31, 32, 34, 50 © William T. Clements Library, University of Michigan; pp. 5, 9 © Burstein Collection/Corbis; p. 10 © Archivo Iconografico, S.A./Corbis; pp. 14, 18, 41, 42 courtesy of the Library of Congress Prints and Photographs Division, Wahington, D.C.; pp. 19, 20, 28 © Independence National Historical Park; p. 21 © The New York Public Library, The Picture Collection; p. 23 courtesy of the Library of Congress, Geography and Map Division; pp. 29, 37 © Hulton Archive/Getty Images; p. 45 Library of Congress, Music Division; pp. 48, 55 © New-York Historical Society, New York/Bridgeman Art Library; p. 52 © National Archives and Records Administration.

Designer: Nelson Sá; Editor: Christine Poolos; Photo Researcher: Adriana Skura